W9-BWF-358

DATE DUE

Zebras

Striped Grass-Grazers

by Lola M. Schaefer

Consultant:
Becky Bishop
Plains Keeper
Indianapolis Zoo

Bridgestone Books
an imprint of Capstone Press
Mankato, Minnesota

Bridgestone Books are published by Capstone Press
151 Good Counsel Drive, P.O. Box 669, Mankato, Minnesota 56002
http://www.capstone-press.com

Library of Congress Cataloging-in-Publication Data
Schaefer, Lola M., 1950–
   Zebras: striped grass-grazers/by Lola M. Schaefer.
   p. cm.—(The wild world of animals)
   Includes bibliographical references and index.
   ISBN 0-7368-0968-6
   1. Zebras—Juvenile literature. [1. Zebras.] I. Title. II. Series.
QL737.U62 S29 2002
599.665'7—dc21   00-012582

Summary: An introduction to zebras describing their physical characteristics, habitat, young,
    food, predators, and relationship to people.

Editorial Credits
Karen L. Daas and Tom Adamson, editors; Karen Risch, product planning editor; Linda Clavel,
    designer and illustrator; Heidi Schoof, photo researcher

Photo Credits
Craig Brandt, 6
Digital Stock, 12
James P. Rowan, cover
Joe McDonald, 16
PhotoDisc, Inc., 1, 20
Richard Demler, 4, 10
Robin Brandt, 8, 14
Visuals Unlimited/Joe McDonald, 18

Table of Contents

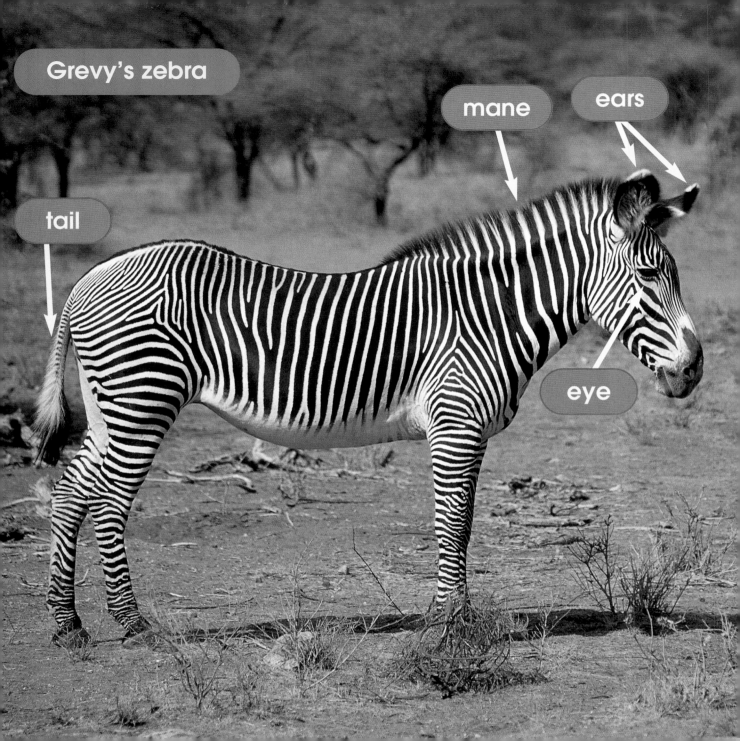

Grevy's zebra

mane

ears

tail

eye

Zebras

Zebras look like horses with black and white stripes. Zebras have short manes and long tails. Adult zebras stand 4 to 5 feet (1.2 to 1.5 meters) tall at the shoulder. They weigh about 600 pounds (272 kilograms).

mane

hair on the head and neck of an animal

plains zebras

FUN FACTS !

No two zebras look exactly alike. Each zebra has a different pattern of stripes.

Zebras Are Mammals

Zebras are mammals. Mammals are warm-blooded animals with a backbone. Adult female zebras give birth to live young. Mothers feed milk to their young.

warm-blooded
having a body temperature that stays the same

mountain zebra

A Zebra's Habitat

All wild zebras live in Africa. Different types of zebras have different habitats. Grevy's zebras make their homes in dry, dusty areas. Plains zebras live in grassy areas. Mountain zebras live in hilly areas. Zebras spend much of their time grazing in long grass.

habitat
the place where an animal lives

Grevy's zebras

What Do Zebras Eat?

Zebras are herbivores. They only eat plants such as grass. Zebras have sharp front teeth to cut the grass. They chew the grass with their flat back teeth. Zebras graze for almost 18 hours each day.

plains zebras

FUN FACTS! Zebras often stand in groups. Their stripes confuse predators. The predators cannot tell how many zebras are in one group.

A Zebra's Stripes

All zebras have stripes on their body. Some zebras have stripes that cover their entire body. Other zebras do not have stripes on their legs. Adult zebras have black and white stripes. Young zebras usually have brown and white stripes.

plains zebras

Mating and Birth

Zebras live in herds. Male zebras are stallions. Female zebras are mares. The head stallion mates with mares in the herd. A young zebra then grows inside its mother for about 13 months. Mares usually give birth to one zebra at a time.

mate
to join together to produce young

plains zebras

FUN FACTS Zebras have very good hearing. They can twist their ears around to listen to sounds from almost any direction.

Foals

Young zebras are foals. A foal can stand 15 minutes after it is born. It can walk one hour after it is born. A newborn foal weighs about 70 pounds (32 kilograms). A foal stays with its mother for about three years.

Two zebras may stand next to each other and face opposite directions. The zebras then can see predators coming from any direction.

plains zebras

Predators

Zebras have many predators. Lions, leopards, cheetahs, wild dogs, and crocodiles kill zebras for food. People also hunt zebras. Hunters kill zebras for their striped hides. Zebras stand in groups to protect themselves from predators.

hide
an animal's skin

plains zebras

Words to Know

endangered (en-DAYN-jurd)—at risk of dying out; some kinds of zebras are endangered.

habitat (HAB-uh-tat)—the place where an animal lives

herbivore (HUR-buh-vor)—an animal that eats only plants

mammal (MAM-uhl)—a warm-blooded animal that has a backbone and feeds milk to its young

mate (MATE)—to join together to produce young

predator (PRED-uh-tur)—an animal that hunts and kills other animals for food

warm-blooded (warm-BLUHD-id)—having a body temperature that stays the same

Read More

Denis-Huot, Christine. *The Zebra, Striped Horse.* Animal Close-Ups. Watertown, Mass.: Charlesbridge, 1999.

Holmes, Kevin J. *Zebras.* Animals. Mankato, Minn.: Bridgestone Books, 2000.

Markert, Jenny. *Zebras.* Chanhassen, Minn.: Child's World, 2001.

Internet Sites

Grevy's Zebra
http://www.sazoo-aq.org/grezebra.html
Plains Zebra
http://www.pbs.org/kratts/world/africa/zebra/index.html
Zebra Information Project
http://www.planet-pets.com/plntzbra.htm

Index